Manatees

by Martha E. H. Rustad

Consulting Editor: Gail Saunders-Smith, Ph.D.

Consultant: Jody Rake, Science Writer,
SeaWorld Education Department

Pebble Books

an imprint of Capstone Press
Mankato, Minnesota

Pebble Books are published by Capstone Press
1710 Roe Crest Drive, North Mankato, Minnesota 56003
www.capstonepub.com

Printed in China by Nordica.
1212/CA21201635
122012   007060R

Library of Congress Cataloging-in-Publication Data
Rustad, Martha E. H. (Martha Elizabeth Hillman), 1975–
   Manatees/by Martha E. H. Rustad.
   p. cm.—(Ocean life)
   Summary: Simple text and photographs describe the physical characteristics
and behavior of manatees.
   Includes bibliographical references (p. 23) and index.
   ISBN-13: 978-0-7368-1657-1 (hardcover)
   ISBN-10: 0-7368-1657-7 (hardcover)
   ISBN-13: 978-0-7368-3414-8 (softcover pbk.)
   ISBN-10: 0-7368-3414-1 (softcover pbk.)
   1. Manatees—Juvenile literature. [1. Manatees.] I. Title. II. Series.
QL737.S63 R87 2003
599.55—dc21
                                            2002014775

Note to Parents and Teachers

The Ocean Life series supports national science standards for units
on the diversity and unity of life. The series shows that animals
have features that help them live in different environments. This
book describes manatees and illustrates how they live. The
photographs support early readers in understanding the text. The
repetition of words and phrases helps early readers learn new
words. This book also introduces early readers to subject-specific
vocabulary words, which are defined in the Words to Know section.
Early readers may need assistance to read some words and to use
the Table of Contents, Words to Know, Read More, Internet Sites,
and Index/Word List sections of the book.

Table of Contents

Manatees are mammals.
Manatees live in oceans
and rivers.

Manatees close
their nostrils underwater.

Manatees lift their nose
out of the water
to breathe air.

Manatees eat plants.

Manatees have a large upper lip. They use their lip to move food into their mouth.

Manatees have a large body and a small head.

tail

flippers

Manatees have a flat tail.
They have two flippers.

Young manatees drink milk from their mother's body.

Manatees play together.

Words to Know

breathe—to take air in and out of the lungs; manatees lift their nose out of the water to breathe; manatees can stay underwater for up to 20 minutes.

flipper—a flat limb with bones found on a sea animal; manatees use their flippers to steer and to move plants to their mouth to eat.

mammal—a warm-blooded animal with a backbone; female mammals feed milk to their young.

nostril—an opening in an animal's nose; air travels to the lungs through the nostrils; manatees close their nostrils to stop water from entering them.

Read More

Klingel, Cynthia Fitterer, and Robert B. Noyed.
Manatees. Wonder Books. Chanhassen, Minn.: Child's World, 2002.

Richardson, Adele. *Manatees: Peaceful Plant-Eaters.* Wild World of Animals. Mankato, Minn.: Bridgestone Books, 2003.

Internet Sites

Track down many sites about manatees.
Visit the FACT HOUND at *http://www.facthound.com*

IT IS EASY! IT IS FUN!

1) Go to *http://www.facthound.com*
2) Type in: 0736816577

3) Click on "FETCH IT" and FACT HOUND will find several links hand-picked by our editors.

Relax and let our pal FACT HOUND do the research for you!

Index/Word List

Word Count: 73
Early-Intervention Level: 9

Credits

Steve Christensen, cover designer and illustrator; Patrick D. Dentinger, production designer; Kelly Garvin, photo researcher

Avampini—V&W/Bruce Coleman Inc., 4
Colla—V&W/Bruce Coleman Inc., cover, 14, 16
Digital Stock/Marty Snyderman, 8
Jeff Rotman, 1, 18, 20
Paul Sutherland Photography/sutherlandstock.com, 6
Tom Stack & Associates/Timothy O'Keefe, 10; Brian Parker, 12